BLESSINGS, *My* CHILD

101 Blessings for Children

Ginger Payne

BLESSINGS, *My* CHILD

Illumify Media Group
www.IllumifyMedia.com
"We Make Your Writing Shine"

Images © Dreamstime.com

Paperback ISBN: 978-1-947360-00-6
eBook ISBN: 978-1-947360-01-3

Printed in the United States of America
16 17 18 19 20 21 LSI 9 8 7 6 5 4 3 2 1

Acknowledgements

The acknowledgements tend to be the part of a book people skip over (understandable!), but they are the part of the book an author would not be here without.

I want to thank Michael J. Klassen of Illumify Media Group for being at the right place at the right time for me. His publishing and editing help have been invaluable.

Images ©Dreamstime.com provided a wonderful resource for finding just the right stock photo I wanted for each blessing.

Jeff Goehring bravely took on the job of turning 101 photos into illustrations. Thank you, Jeff.

Much appreciation to my daughter, Kristy Matteson, for her help and counsel with online design and marketing.

My final thanks is my most significant. My husband, Chris, has been an amazing advisor, hands-on helper and cheerleader from the start of this project to the end. He is one of the most incredible gifts God provided when I told God I needed help.

Dedication

This book is dedicated
to my four precious grandchildren,
J. D., Sean, Bella, and Connor,
who helped inspire me to put
these blessings into print.

From the Author

*J*his project began, without my realization, many years ago when I was asked to write a blessing based on Scripture for every woman attending a women's conference. Then three years ago, I wrote a blessing for every child living at two Children of Hope homes for children in Kenya that my husband and I help support. (www.cohafrica.org)

Both projects blessed me in so many ways. What a delight to read Scripture and discover the creative methods God uses to bless us. His love is incomparable! I continued writing children's blessings whenever I had a chance, because I love children and truly want children to feel blessed by their Lord.

God started "talking" to me about leaving a legacy for children after I attended an impactful seminar. That following summer brought some unexpected events into my life that caused me to put this project on the back burner. But God kept whispering. I then participated in two back-to-back Bible studies where God continued to speak, only now with a louder voice about what HE wanted me to pursue.

After telling the Lord I wanted to obey his leading and letting Him know I only could do this with His help, doors started to open in amazing ways that led to this finished project.

My heartfelt desire is that children and the important adults in their lives will be blessed in incredible ways by reading and discussing this book together, one or two blessings at a time, getting to know God and each other even better.

May God bless your time together!

Ginger Payne

Mark 10:16 (NIV)

And he took the children in his arms, put his hands on them and blessed them.

Children Are Special to Me

Beloved Child,
You are so special to
me. I have always
treasured My loved younger ones.
You are willing to see Me and believe.
~ *Your loving Jesus*

---

1. Did you know how much I talk about how special children are to Me in the Bible?
2. Why do you think I love children so much?
3. What can you do better than grown-ups?

John 15:9 (NIV)

As the Father has loved me, so have I loved you.
Now remain in my love.

Be at Home with Me

My Child,
I love you as much as God loves Me.
Be at home in My love.
Love always!
~ *Jesus*

1. How much do you think God loves Me?
2. Can you believe I love you that much?
3. What does it mean to be at home in My love?

1 John 4:18

There is no fear in love. Instead perfect love drives away fear. Fear has to do with being punished. The one who fears does not have perfect love.

3

No Fear in My Love

Loving Child,
I want to fill you with My perfect love,
so that you do not have to fear.
My love always wants
what is best for you.
~ *Your precious Lord Jesus*

1. Why do you think My love is perfect?
2. If love is perfect, why don't you need to fear?
3. Is it easy to have perfect love?

Isaiah 45:2

I will march out ahead of you. I will make the mountains level. I will break down bronze gates. I will cut through their heavy bars.

～～～ 4 ～～～

Help
in the Hard Places

Dear One,
I will help you when life is hard,
and when problems seem
to block your way.
~ *Your loving Helper, God*

～～～～～～～～

1. In My Scripture verse today, what do mountains, bronze gates and heavy bars have in common?
2. What are some problems you feel are blocking your way?
3. Why is it good to have Me marching ahead of you?

Ephesians 1:18–19

I pray that you may understand more clearly. Then you will know the hope God has chosen you to receive. . . . And you will know God's great power. It can't be compared with anything else. His power works for us who believe. It is the same mighty strength.

My Power for You

Sweet Child,
I want you to know Me personally,
so that you will know all the things
I am calling you to do.
You will have My power to help you;
the same power I used
to bring Jesus back to life.
~ *Love always. God*

᠅᠉᠅᠉᠅᠉᠅᠉᠅᠉᠅᠉

1. What does it mean to know someone personally?
2. Why do I want you to know Me personally?
3. How much power do you think I have?

Psalm 139:17–18

God, your thoughts about me are priceless. No one can possibly add them all up. If I could count them, they would be more than the grains of sand. If I were to fall asleep counting and then wake up you would still be there with me.

My Thoughts About You

Priceless Child,
I think about you all the time.
You would never be able to count
all the times I think about you.
It is more than all the grains
of sand on the Earth.
I start each day thinking about you.
Love you!
~ God

~~~~~~~~~~~

1. How many grains of sand do you think are on the Earth?
2. Would you ever be able to count them all?
3. How can you know I am thinking about you all the time?

Isaiah 40:28

Don't you know who made everything? Haven't you heard about him? The Lord is the God who lives forever. He created everything on earth. He won't become worn out or get tired. No one will ever know how great his understanding is.

Never Tired

Sweet One,
I am your God who lives forever
and I never get tired.
I am always awake to help you
with anything.
I created everything and
know all things.
I promise.
~ *Your Heavenly Father*

~~~~~~~~~~

1. Did you know that I never get tired or need to sleep?
2. Why do think I never get tired?
3. How much energy do you think it took for Me to create everything on Earth?

Psalm 23:1, 4

The Lord is my shepherd. He gives me everything
I need. . . . Even though I walk through the darkest
valley, I will not be afraid. You are with me. Your
shepherd's rod and staff comfort me.

Your Loving Shepherd

Child,
I am your loving Shepherd.
I care about you and I
meet your needs.
I don't want you to fear anything,
even when times are not good,
for I am ALWAYS with you.
Love,
~ Jesus

---

1. What are ways a shepherd takes care of his sheep?
2. Do you think I am a good Shepherd?
3. When are times you've been glad to have Me as your Shepherd caring for you?

Romans 8:28 (NIV)

And we know that in all things God works for the
good of those who love him, who have been called
according to his purpose.

For Your Good Always

My Special Child,
God causes everything to work
together
for your good,
if you love Him and want
to understand
His purposes for you.
I promise.

~ *Jesus*

---

1. Do you think I work things together for your good?
2. Does it always feel like things are good?
3. Why would I know what is better for you than you do?

Joshua 1:5 (NIV)

No one will be able to stand up against you all the days of your life. As I was with Moses, so I will be with you; I will never leave you nor forsake you.

I Will Never Leave

Dear One,
I will always be with you.
I will never leave you
or walk away from you.
All my love,
~ God

---

1. Do you get sad sometimes when people leave you?
2. How is it possible that I will never leave you?
3. What do you think about My always being with you, even though you can't see Me?

Philippians 4:6

Don't worry about anything. No matter what happens, tell God about everything. Ask and pray, and give thanks to him.

11

Pray About Everything

My Dear Child,
I don't want you to worry
about anything.
Instead, I want you to pray
to Me about everything.
Tell Me what you need,
and remember
to thank Me for all I have done.
~ *Your loving Lord Jesus*

1. How does it feel when you worry?
2. Why is it better to pray to Me when you are worried about something?
3. Do you remember to thank Me when I answer your prayers?

John 1:23 (NIV)

John replied in the words of Isaiah the prophet,
"I am the voice of one calling in the desert, 'Make
straight the way for the Lord.'"

Prepare the Way

Child,
prepare the way for
Me to come into your life.
Love,
~ Jesus

---

1. How can you prepare for Me to come into your life?
2. Would you like to have Me in your life?
3. How can I help in everyone's life?

John 1:29 (NIV)

The next day John saw Jesus coming toward him
and said, "Look, the Lamb of God, who takes away
the sin of the world!"

Lamb of God

Beloved Child,
I am the Lamb of God
who takes away the sins of the world,
including yours.
I love you so much!
~ *Jesus*

1. What does it mean to sin?
2. Why did you need Me to take away your sins for you?
3. What are some sins you want to thank Me for taking away from you?

1 John 1:5, 7 (NIV)

This is the message we have heard from him and declare to you: God is light; in him there is no darkness at all. But if we walk in the light, as he is in the light, we have fellowship with one another, and the blood of Jesus, his Son, purifies us from all sin.

No Darkness

My Child,
God is light. In fact,
in God there is no darkness at all.
If we walk in God's light,
we can share in His
wonderful light all together.
God's light took away all of our sins.
You can trust God!
I know that, because I am His Son.
~ Jesus

1. Do you like knowing there is no darkness in Me?
2. What happens to darkness when light shows up?
3. How can you walk in My light?

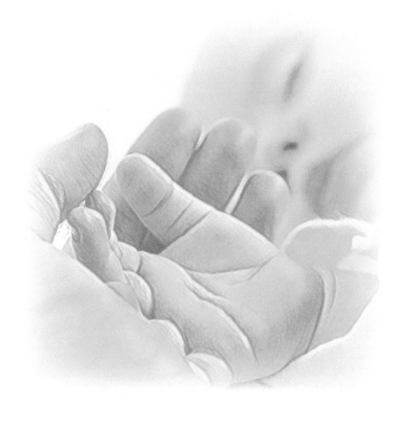

Psalm 145:8-9

The Lord is gracious, kind and tender.
He is slow to get angry and full of love.
The Lord is good to all. He shows deep concern for
everything he has made.

15

My Love Is Best

For you Sweet One,
I am full of love, slow to get angry
and I will show tenderness to you.
Love,
~ *Your Heavenly Father*

❦❦❦❦❦❦❦❦

1. Do you like it when someone is slow to get angry with you?
2. What does it mean if someone shows tenderness to you?
3. What are ways I show My love to you?

Psalm 138:3

When I called out to you, you answered me.
You made me strong and brave.

Pray Always

Dear Child,
when you pray, I will answer you.
I can help you be strong and brave.
I promise.
~ God

1. When do you like to pray?
2. What does it feel like to be strong and brave?
3. Do you remember to ask Me to give you strength when you need it?

Psalm 143:8 (NIV)

Let the morning bring me word of your unfailing love, for I have put my trust in you. Show me the way I should go, for to you I lift up my soul.

Wake Up with Me

Special One,
Trust in Me when you first wake up,
and offer me your heart and soul,
and I will show you the way to go.

My love never fails.
Love,
~ God

～ゟ～ゟ～ゟ～ゟ～ゟ～ゟ

1. Why do I want you to offer Me your heart?
2. What is your soul?
3. How can you start your day trusting Me?

Psalm 121:7-8

The Lord will keep you from every kind of harm.
He will watch over your life. The Lord will watch
over your life no matter where you go, both now
and forever.

Safe with Me

My Child,
I will keep you from harm
and watch over your life.
I will guard you no matter
where you are going.
~ *Your loving Heavenly Father*

1. What does it mean to guard someone?
2. Are you glad I will guard you no matter where you are?
3. What are some things you would like to be guarded from?

Psalm 34:17

Godly people cry out, and the Lord hears them. He saves them from all their troubles.

Always Listening

Loved One,
I hear you when you call to Me.
I am always listening and
I want to help you.
I promise with love.
~ God

≈≈≈≈≈≈≈≈≈

1. How do you call to Me?
2. Do you think I am always listening to you?
3. When are some times you want My help?

1 John 4:13 (NIV)

We know that we live in him and he in us, because he has given us of his Spirit.

20

God's Spirit

My Child,
you live in God and
He lives in you because
God has given you His Spirit.
Love always,
~ Jesus

~~~~~~~~~~

1. How can you live in Me and I live in you?
2. Who is My Spirit?
3. How does My Spirit help you by living in you?

Psalm 84:11–12

The Lord God is like the sun that gives us light. He is like a shield that keeps us safe. The Lord blesses us with favor and honor. He doesn't hold back anything good from those whose lives are without blame. Lord who rules over all, blessed is the person who trusts in you.

I Am Your Sunshine

Dear Child,
I am your sunshine and
your protection.
I love to give you gifts of all kinds.
I will not hold back good
things from you.
You will be blessed because
you trust in Me.
I promise.
~ Your loving Heavenly Father

᠅᠅᠅᠅᠅᠅᠅

1. What kinds of gifts do I give you?
2. Why do you think I love to give you good things?
3. Why are you blessed if you trust in Me?

Philippians 4:13 (NIV)

I can do everything through him who gives me strength.

22

Let Me Help

Dear One,
you can do all you need
to do with My help.
I will give you the strength.
I promise.

~ Jesus

1. Are there times when you need help?
2. What are some times when you feel you need the most help?
3. How can you count on Me for that help?

Psalm 138:8

Lord, you will show that I was right to trust you.
Lord, your faithful love continues forever. You have
done so much for us, so don't stop now.

My Purpose for You

My Child,
I will accomplish my
purposes for you.
I will never give up on you.
You are the work of My hands,
and My love for you lasts forever.
~ *Your Best Friend, God*

---

1. How are you the work of My hands?
2. What purposes do you think I have for you?
3. What is one purpose you know I have for you right now?

John 15:12 (NIV)

My command is this: Love each other as I have loved you.

24

Love One Another

Dear One,
My desire is that you love each other
the same way that I love you.
It is the best way to love.
I love you deeply.

~ *Jesus*

1. How have I shown My love for you?
2. Why is My way of loving the best way to love?
3. What are ways you can love like Me?

Psalm 106:1

Praise the Lord. Give thanks to the Lord, because he is good. His faithful love continues forever.

Praise the Lord

Sweet Child,
It blesses Me when you praise Me!
Say, "thank you" to Me, for I am good.
My trustworthy love lasts forever.
Love always,
~ God

1. How can you praise Me?
2. Do you thank Me for My goodness?
3. How does it make you feel to know My love for you lasts forever?

John 1:4–5

Life was in him, and that life was the light for all people. The light shines in the darkness. But the darkness has not overcome the light.

26

I Am The Light

Child,
I am the light that shines
in the darkness.
I am your light.
Love,
~ Jesus

⚘⚘⚘⚘⚘⚘⚘

1. What are some ways I can be your light?
2. Why do you think My light wins over darkness?
3. Why does having light make you feel better than when things are dark?

Psalm 144:2 (NIV)

He is my loving God and my fortress,
my stronghold and my deliverer,
my shield, in whom I take refuge,
who subdues peoples under me.

27

I Am Your Fortress

Dear One,
God is your loving friend,
your fortress, your tower of safety,
your rescuer. He is your shield,
and you can take shelter in Him.
I promise.

~ *Jesus*

---

1. What is a fortress?
2. How does a shield protect you?
3. When are you glad I am your shield and rescuer?

1 John 2:5–6 (NIV)

But if anyone obeys his word, love for God is truly made complete in them. This is how we know we are in him: Whoever claims to live in him must live as Jesus did.

28

Obey My Words

Sweet Child,
if you obey what My Word says,
My love is truly made
complete in you.
Then I can help you live a life
like I lived on Earth.
I'm always here to help you.

~ *Jesus*

1. How can you obey the Bible?
2. What kind of life did I live while I was here on Earth?
3. Why is it important to know what the Bible says?

2 Corinthians 12:9

But he said to me, "My grace is all you need. My power is strongest when you are weak." So I am very happy to brag about how weak I am. Then Christ's power can rest on me.

29

Strong When You Are Weak

Child,
Do not fear when you feel weak,
because you can rely on My power
to help you.
My power is the strongest
in the world.
Love,
~ *Christ Jesus*

1. What does it feel like to be weak?
2. Why can My power be stronger when you feel weak?
3. How can My power help you?

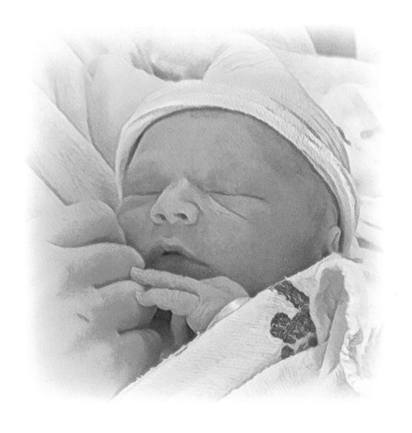

John 1:13

To be a child of God has nothing to do with human parents. Children of God are not born because of human choice or because a husband wants them to be born. They are born because of what God does.

30

You Are My Child

Dear One,

You are a child of God
because you received Me.
Love,
~ Jesus

~~~~~~~~~~~~~~

1. Do you think you can be a child of God as well as someone else's child?
2. Do you think My Father is a good parent?
3. When are times you are glad My Father is your parent?

Deuteronomy 31:8

The Lord himself will go ahead of you. He will be with you. He will never leave you. He'll never desert you. So don't be afraid. Don't lose hope.

31

I Am Right Here

Dear Child,
I am walking ahead of you.
I am also right here beside you.
I will never leave you.
So, you do not need to be afraid
or lose hope.
I promise.
~ *Your Loving God*

~~~~~~~~~~

1. What makes you afraid?
2. How do you feel knowing I am with you and watching out for you?
3. What does it mean that I will never leave you?

Psalm 119:105

Your word is like a lamp that shows me the way. It is like a light that guides me.

32

I Will Guide You

Special One,
the words of the Bible
can help guide you in
everything you do.
I can show you the way to go.
Love,
~ Your Heavenly Father

~~~~~~~~~~~~~~

1. How can words in the Bible be a lamp and a light?
2. Do you think it is good to know the words in the Bible?
3. Why do you think I wanted you to have the Bible?

Mark 10:27

Jesus looked at them and said, "With people this is impossible, but not with God. All things are possible with God."

33

All Things Are Possible

My Dear Child,
even if you think something
can't be done,
remember that all things are
possible with My help.
Trust Me.
~ *Jesus.*

~~~~~~~~~~~~~

1. What are things in your life you think can't be done?
2. Do you think if you ask Me I can help you with those things?
3. How would you like Me to help you right now?

Psalm 130:7

Israel, put your hope in the Lord, because the Lord's love never fails. He sets his people completely free.

34

Unfailing Love

Look and see, My Child,
My love is unfailing and
I want to set you free.
I love you.
~ God

---

1. When love is unfailing, what kind of love is it?
2. What does it mean to be free?
3. How do you feel when you are not free?

Psalm 144:15 (NIV)

Blessed are the people of whom this is true;
blessed are the people whose God is the Lord.

You Will Be Blessed

Beloved Child,
you are blessed because
I am your God and your Lord.
I promise with love.

~ *God*

---

1. What does it mean to be blessed?
2. How are you blessed by having Me as your Lord?
3. Do you wish everyone could know Me?

John 8:47

Whoever belongs to God hears what God says.
The reason you don't hear is that you don't
belong to God.

36

Can You Hear Me?

Dear One,
when you belong to Me,
you can hear what I say.
I want you to belong to Me
so I can guide and help you.
You can trust Me!
Love,
~ God

1. What does it mean to belong to Me?
2. Do you want to hear what I say to you?
3. What are ways you can hear Me speak to you?

John 10:28

I give them eternal life, and they will never die. No one will steal them out of my hand.

Life That Lasts Forever

Special One,
I want to give you a life
that lasts forever with Me in heaven
so you will never really die.
No one can steal you away from me.
Love,
~ Jesus

❧❦❧❦❧❦❧❦❧❦

1. Did you know I want you to live in heaven with Me forever?
2. What does it mean that you will never really die?
3. Why can no one can steal you away from Me?

Jeremiah 29:13 (NIV)

You will seek me and find me when you seek me
with all your heart.

38

Look for Me

My Child,
if you look for me with all your heart,
you will find Me.
I promise.
~ God

---

1. When you look for something with all of your heart, how hard are you looking?
2. Have you looked for Me with all your heart?
3. Why do you think I want you to look for Me?

Colossians 3:13–14

Put up with one another. Forgive one another
if you are holding something against someone.
Forgive, just as the Lord forgave you. And over all
these good things put on love. Love holds them all
together perfectly as if they were one.

39

Forgiven to Forgive

Dear One,
it is so important for you
to forgive others
just as much as I have forgiven you,
which is always and totally!
And most importantly, show love
to all those around you.
Love is what I want most
for My children.
I love you always.

~ Jesus

1. Is it always easy to forgive those who have hurt you?
2. Why is it important that you forgive?
3. Is there someone you would like to forgive for hurting you?

1 Thessalonians 5:16–18

Always be joyful. Never stop praying. Give thanks no matter what happens. God wants you to thank him because you believe in Christ Jesus.

40

Always Thankful

Sweet One,
My desire for you is that
you will always be cheerful,
that you will want to talk to Me
all the time,
and that you will be able to thank Me,
no matter what.
I love you!
~ *Jesus*

---

1. When is it hard to be cheerful?
2. How can you talk to Me all the time?
3. What are ways you still can be thankful, even when everything isn't going your way?

2 Peter 1:2

May more and more grace and peace be given to you. May they come to you as you learn more about God and about Jesus our Lord.

41

My Peace for You

My Child,
it is My wish
for My grace and peace
to spill over into your life.
Love,
~ Jesus

---

1. What do you think the word grace means?
2. How can you show grace in your life?
3. If something is spilling over in your life, how much of it is there?

John 1:39

"Come," he replied. "You will see." So they went and saw where he was staying. They spent the rest of the day with him. It was about four o'clock in the afternoon.

42

Come Be with Me

Dear One,
come and spend
your day with me.
I love you.

~ Jesus

❧❧❧❧❧❧❧❧

1. Where do you think I live?
2. Do you have to see Me to spend time with Me?
3. How can you spend time with Me?

Isaiah 41:10

So do not be afraid. I am with you. Do not be terrified. I am your God. I will make you strong and help you. I will hold you safe in my hands. I always do what is right.

I Am Your God

My Special Child,
don't be afraid, for I am
always with you.
Don't be sad, because I am your God.
I will give you the strength you need
and I will help you.
I will hold on tightly to you.
I promise.
~ Your Heavenly Father

~~~~~~~~~~~~

1. What makes you sad?
2. When do you feel afraid?
3. Did you know I am always there to help you
   whenever you feel sad or afraid?

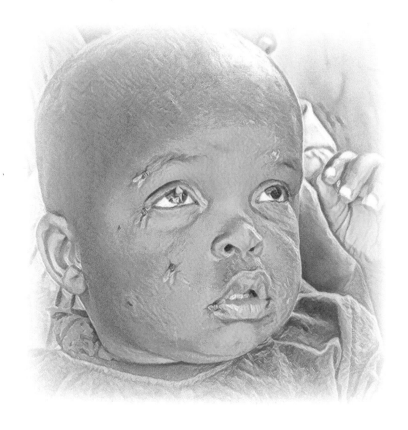

Psalm 86:5–7

Lord, you are forgiving and good. You are full of love
for all who call out to you. Lord, hear my prayer.
Listen to my cry for mercy. When I'm in trouble, I
will call out to you. And you will answer me.

44

Mercy is Yours

Dear One,

I am forgiving and good.

I love you and I will answer you

when you call to Me in

your times of trouble.

I will hear your cries for mercy.

Love always,

~ God

～⚬～⚬～⚬～⚬～⚬～⚬

1. What does it mean to cry for mercy?
2. Do you think about calling on Me when you're in trouble?
3. What are some ways you'd like mercy from Me?

1 Peter 3:12 (NIV)

For the eyes of the Lord are on the righteous and his ears are attentive to their prayer, but the face of the Lord is against those who do evil.

I Hear You

Dear Child,
My eyes are watching over you and
My ears are attentive
to your prayers.
I love you.

~ *Jesus*

꘡꘡꘡꘡꘡꘡꘡꘡꘡

1. Are you glad that I am watching over you?
2. What does it mean that I am "attentive to your prayers"?
3. Why is it nice when people listen to you?

Colossians 1:15

The Son is the exact likeness of God, who can't be
seen. The Son is first, and he is over all creation.

46

I Created Everything

Sweet Child,
when you look at Me and
My time on Earth,
you get a good idea of
what God is like.
I created all things,
both in heaven and on Earth.
I gave all things their purpose.
I give you My purpose as well.
Love,
~ Jesus

---

1. How can you know God by knowing Me?
2. What are some things I created?
3. What are some things you think I still want to create in your life?

Lamentations 3:22-23

The Lord loves us very much. So we haven't been completely destroyed. His loving concern never fails. His great love is new every morning. Lord, how faithful you are!

47

New Every Day

Special Child,
My faithful love never runs out.
My tender love cannot dry up.
My love for you is
created new for you every morning.
I honor what I say.
I promise with love.
~ Your Heavenly Father

~~~~~~~~~~~~~~~

1. What kind of love never runs out or dries up?
2. When something is created new, is it usually fresh and different?
3. What does it mean to honor what you say?

Psalm 140:6–7

I say to the Lord, "You are my God." Lord, hear my cry for mercy. Lord and King, you save me because you are strong. You are like a shield that keeps me safe in the day of battle.

48

I Can Help You

Dear One,
I hear your cry for help.
I am your Strong Helper.
Blessings and love always,
~ God

---

1. What does it mean that I am a Strong Helper?
2. When do you cry to Me for help?
3. How can you be sure I hear your cry for help?

1 John 2:8–10

But I am writing what amounts to a new command. Its truth was shown in how Jesus lived. It is also shown in how you live. That's because the darkness is passing away. And the true light is already shining. Suppose someone claims to be in the light but hates a brother or sister. Then they are still in the darkness. Anyone who loves their brother and sister lives in the light. There is nothing in them to make them fall into sin.

❀❀ 49 ❀❀

Come to My Light

Child,
because of Me, the
darkness is passing
and the true light is already shining.
To be part of the true light,
you must love your brothers
and your sisters.
Otherwise, you will be
part of the darkness.
I bring you light and love.

~ Jesus

---

1. Who are your brothers and sisters?
2. Does it sometimes feel dark when you are mean and unloving to others?
3. How can I help you love better and enjoy the light I bring to you?

Ephesians 2:10

We are God's creation. He created us to belong to Christ Jesus. Now we can do good works. Long ago God prepared these works for us to do.

Your Helper and Friend

Dear One,
you are My prized Child.
I created you to be My special helper,
so you can do the good things
I planned for you long ago.
You are my loved helper and friend.

~ Jesus

---

1. What does it mean to be prized?
2. Do you want to be My helper?
3. What are ways you can be My helper?

John 14:1 (NIV)

Do not let your hearts be troubled. You believe in
God; believe also in me.

Trust in Me

My Child,
don't let your heart
be afraid or confused.
You can trust in God,
and you also can trust in Me.
I really love you.

~ Jesus

---

1. What does it feel like when your heart is afraid or confused?
2. How can trusting Me help that feeling?
3. Why do you think I don't want you to be afraid or confused?

1 John 4:10

Here is what love is. It is not that we loved God. It is that he loved us and sent his Son to give his life to pay for our sins.

52

Your Saving Gift

Child,
this is love;
that God sent Me as a
saving gift for your sins.
I love you that much!

~ Jesus

≈≈≈≈≈≈≈

1. What does it mean to be given a gift?
2. What was the saving gift I gave to you?
3. Do you think that was easy for Me?

Mark 12:30 (NIV)

Love the Lord your God with all your heart and with all your soul and with all your mind and with all your strength.

Love Me
with All of You

My Chosen Child,
it is my wish that you
love Me with all your heart,
with all your soul, with all your mind
and with all your strength.
This is how I love you.

~ Jesus

～⟡～⟡～⟡～⟡～⟡～

1. How can you love Me with your mind?
2. What are ways you can love Me with all your strength?
3. Did you know that this is how much I love you?

Psalm 16:7–8

I will praise the Lord. He gives me good advice.
Even at night my heart teaches me. I keep my eyes
always on the Lord. He is at my right hand. So I
will always be secure.

54

Always with You

Dear One,
I am giving you wise advice
both day and night.
I want to help you wherever you go.
You will be alright,
for I am right beside you.
I love you.
~ God

1. What does it mean to receive wise advice?
2. Do you think I am full of wise advice?
3. What is some wise advice I can give you right now?

Psalm 66:5

Come and see what God has done. See what
wonderful things he has done for people!

55

My Wonders

Child,
come and see what I have done,
what wonderful things
I do for My children!
You are loved by Me.

~ God

---

1. What are ways you can see the things I have done?
2. How have you seen My wonders in your life?
3. What is the best thing I have done for you?

John 16:33 (NIV)

I have told you these things, so that in me you may have peace. In this world you will have trouble. But take heart! I have overcome the world.

56

I Overcome All

My Dear Child,
here on this Earth you will have
many hard and sad times.
But you can be hopeful,
because I have overcome the world.
I am always here for you.

~ Jesus

❧❧❧❧❧❧❧❧

1. What does it mean that I have overcome the world?
2. Will you still have sad times while living here on Earth?
3. When do you think your sad times will be over for good?

Colossians 3:12 (NIV)

Therefore, as God's chosen people, holy and dearly loved, clothe yourselves with compassion, kindness, humility, gentleness and patience.

57

My Desire for You

My Loved Child,
you are blessed and
dearly loved by Me.
Let me fill you with My
love, kindness,
humility, gentleness, and patience.
Love,
~ Jesus

1. What does it mean to be patient?
2. What does it mean to have humility?
3. Why do I want them in your life?

Psalm 130:5–6

With all my heart I wait for the Lord to help me. I put my hope in his word. I wait for the Lord to help me. I want his help more than night watchmen want the morning to come. I'll say it again. I want his help more than might watchmen want the morning to come.

58

Wait and Watch for Me

Child,
Pray to Me and wait for Me
to tell you which way to go.
Keep watching and waiting
to hear from Me.
I will answer when the time is right.
I love you.

~ God

1. Is it always easy to wait?
2. Why do we sometimes need to wait for something to happen?
3. What are ways I let you know the best thing to do?

Psalm 145:14

The Lord takes good care of all those who fall. He lifts up all those who feel helpless.

I'm Here When You Need Me

Special One,
I will help you when you
are feeling down
and lift you up when you need help.
I do this because I love you.
I promise.
~ God

1. What makes you feel down?
2. When do you need help?
3. How can I can help you if you ask Me?

1 John 5:18

We know that those who are children of God do not keep on sinning. The Son of God keeps them safe. The evil one can't harm them.

I Will Keep You from Evil

Dear One,
because you are My child,
I will keep you safe and
help you to do the right thing,
and not the bad thing.
The evil one cannot harm you.
Love,
~ Jesus

1. What are some right choices I have helped you make?
2. When are some times you chose to do the wrong thing?
3. Who is the "evil one"?

Romans 15:13

May the God who gives hope fill you with great joy.
May you have perfect peace as you trust in him.
May the power of the Holy Spirit fill you with hope.

My Hope in You

Sweet Child,
I want My hope to fill you
to the top with joy and peace,
as you trust in Me.
I want you to be full of hope,
by the power of My Holy Spirit.
I love you!

~ Jesus

1. What does it mean to be "filled to the top"?
2. Does it sound good to be filled to the top with hope and joy and peace?
3. How can My Spirit help you to have hope?

Romans 8:35

Who can separate us from Christ's love? Can trouble or hard times or harm or hunger? Can nakedness or danger of war?

62

Love No Matter What

Dear Child,
nothing and no one can
separate you from My love.
Not trouble, not hard times,
not mean people,
not hunger or danger of any kind.
My love is forever!

~ *Jesus*

❦❦❦❦❦❦❦❦

1. When have you experienced hard times?
2. Are you glad I am with you in all your hard times?
3. What does it mean that My love is forever?

Psalm 91:11–12

The Lord will command his angels to take good care of you. They will lift you up in their hands. Then you won't trip over a stone.

63

Angels on Guard

Dear One,
I will command my angels to
guard you wherever you go.
They will keep you from harm
and lift you up if you fall.
This is how much I love you.
~ God

---

1. Who are My angels?
2. Even though you can't see angels, are they still able to help you?
3. What harm do you want My angels to guard you from?

John 3:17

God did not send his Son into the world to judge the world. He sent his Son to save the world through him.

64

I Came to Save

My Child,
God did not send Me into the world
to judge you, but to save you.
Love,
~ Jesus

---

1. What does it mean to judge someone?
2. If someone judges you, how does it make you feel?
3. Why don't I judge you?

Colossians 1:13-14

He has saved us from the kingdom of darkness.
He has brought us into the kingdom of the Son he
loves. Because of what the Son has done, we have
been set free. Because of him, all of our sins have
been forgiven.

65

God's Kingdom

Beloved Child,
God has saved you from darkness and
has brought you into the kingdom
that I want for you.
In Me you can have life
and forgiveness.
I love you so much.

~ Jesus.

---

1. What do you think My kingdom looks like?
2. Can you have My kingdom here on Earth?
3. Why is it so important that you have been totally forgiven?

Romans 8:31–32

What should we say then? Since God is on our side, who can be against us? God did not spare his own Son. He gave him up for us all. Then won't he also freely give us everything else?

Always on Your Side

Dear One,
with God on your side,
you have everything going for you!
God did not spare His own Son,
but gave Me up to die for you.
He also will gladly do
many more things for you.
God loves you that much.

~ *Jesus*

ᕫᕫᕫᕫᕫᕫ

1. What does it mean that My life wasn't spared?
2. Why do you think I died for you?
3. What other things would you like Me to do for you?

Psalm 147:3

He heals those who have broken hearts. He takes care of their wounds.

Healing from Jesus

My Child,
I will heal your broken heart
and bandage your wounds.
I love you!
~ God

———

1. What breaks your heart and makes you sad?
2. How can I bandage your wounds?
3. What wounds would you like Me to bandage?

Psalm 103:11–12

He loves those who have respect for him.
His love is as high as the heavens are above the
earth. He has removed our sins from us.
He has removed them as far as the east is from the west.

God's Huge Love

Loved Child,
My love for you is huge!
My love is as huge as the
distance from Earth to heaven.
And I have taken away the things
you have done wrong
as far as one side of the whole Earth
is from the other.
That is how much I care for you.
~ God

---

1. If something is huge, how big is it?
2. How far do you think it is from one side of the
   Earth all the way to the other side?
3. Can you believe I love you so much that I want
   to take away all your sins always?

Galatians 5:22-23 (NIV)

But the fruit of the Spirit is love, joy, peace, patience, kindness, goodness, faithfulness, gentleness and self-control. Against such things there is no law.

My Gifts for You

My Child,
My Spirit can give
love, joy, peace, patience, kindness,
goodness, faithfulness,
gentleness, and self-control.
These are wonderful gifts
I want you to have!
Love,
~ Jesus

～६～६～६～६～६～

1. What does it mean to have self-control?
2. Which of the gifts I want for you are the hardest for you?
3. Why is it important for you to have them?

Philippians 4:8

Finally, my brothers and sisters, always think about what is true. Think about what is noble, right and pure. Think about what is lovely and worthy of respect. If anything is excellent or worthy of praise, think about those kinds of things.

70

All Things Excellent

Special One,
fill your thoughts with things that are
true, and respectable,
and right, and good,
and lovely, and pure.
Think about things that are excellent
and worthy of praise.
This pleases Me.
~ Jesus

~~~~~~~~~~

1. What does it mean if something is respectable?
2. What are some things you think are excellent
   and worthy of praise?
3. Why does it please Me for you to fill your mind
   with these things?

1 John 5:14–15

Here is what we can be sure of when we come to God in prayer. If we ask anything in keeping with what he wants, he hears us. If we know that God hears what we ask for, we know that we have it.

71

I Hear and Answer

Child,
you can be sure that
whatever you ask that agrees with
My plan for you, I will
hear and answer.

~ *Your Loving Jesus*

---

1. What does it mean to be sure about something?
2. What are some ways you can know what I want for your life?
3. What do you think I want for you right now?

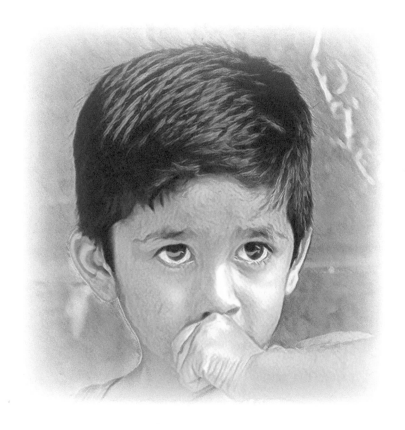

1 Peter 5:6–7

So make yourselves humble. Put yourselves under
God's mighty hand. Then he will honor you at the
right time. Turn all your worries over to him. He
cares about you.

72

Give Me Your Worries

Dear One,
it is best not to think too
highly of yourself.
I will honor you at the right time.
Give Me all your worries,
for I really care about you.
Love Always,
~ Jesus

⸎⸎⸎⸎⸎⸎

1. What are ways you can think too highly of yourself?
2. What does it mean to honor someone?
3. What worries would you like to give Me?

2 Thessalonians 3:3

But the Lord is faithful. He will strengthen you.
He will guard you from the evil one.

73

I Am Your Strength

My Child,
I am faithful and I will
strengthen you.
I will protect you from evil.
I am here for you!

~ Jesus

1. What does it mean to be faithful?
2. What are some things you think are evil?
3. Why do you need Me to protect you from evil?

1 John 5:12

Whoever belongs to the Son has life. Whoever doesn't belong to the Son of God doesn't have life.

Come Have Life

Loved One,
if you have Me,
you have life.
All My love,
~ Jesus

---

1. How can you have Me?
2. What does it mean that you can have life if you have Me?
3. Did you know that with Me you will have life always?

Psalm 126:3 (NIV)

The Lord has done great things for us, and we are filled with joy.

75

Filled with Joy

Sweet Child,
I have done and want to continue to
do great things for you,
so you will be filled with joy.
Love always,
~ God

~~~~~~~~~

1. What great things would you like Me to do for you?
2. Do I always do what you want?
3. Why can you be filled with joy when I do what I
   know is right for you?

Psalm 32:7

You are my hiding place. You will keep me safe from
trouble. You will surround me with songs sung by
those who praise you because you save your people.

76

I Am Your Safe Place

Dear Special One,
I am your safe place to hide.
I will guard you from
danger and trouble.
I will sing songs of
protection over you.
~ *Your loving Heavenly Father*

⌇⌇⌇⌇⌇⌇⌇⌇

1. How can I be a safe place for you to hide?
2. Did you know that I sing songs over you?
3. What do you think My songs sound like?

Isaiah 41:13

I am the Lord your God. I take hold of your right hand. I say to you, "Do not be afraid. I will help you."

77

I Won't Let Go

My Child,
I am your God,
who holds tightly to your hand.
You don't need to be afraid,
because I am not letting go.
I am your God who loves you!

---

1. When you are scared, how does it feel to have someone hold tightly to your hand?
2. Do you hope they won't let go of your hand until you're no longer afraid?
3. If I am holding your hand, why don't you need to be afraid?

John 1:12 (NIV)

Yet to all who received him, to those who believed
in his name, he gave the right to become children
of God.

78

God's Family

Dear Child,
if you believe I am who I say I am,
and if you believe I can
do what I promise.
you are one of My children.
I want you in My family!
Love,
~ Jesus

1. Who do I say that I am?
2. What are some of My promises to you?
3. Are you happy I want you in My family?

Psalm 46:1

God is our place of safety. He gives us strength. He is always there to help us in times of trouble.

Help in Times of Trouble

Dear One,
I am your shelter
and strength. I will be there
to help you whenever
you face trouble.
You can count on Me.
Love,
~ Your Heavenly Father

1. How does a shelter help you?
2. How can I be your shelter and strength?
3. When are times you feel you need a shelter?

1 John 2:2-3

He gave his life to pay for our sins. But he not only paid for our sins. He also paid for the sins of the whole world. We know that we have come to know God if we obey his commands.

80

I Paid the Price

Dearest Child,
I paid the price for your sins
and the sins of the whole world.
I can tell that you know Me
when you obey My commandments.
My commandments are good.
I promise.
~ Jesus

1. What is a commandment?
2. What are some of My commandments?
3. How can you know more of My commandments?

Psalm 13:5-6 (NIV)

But I trust in your unfailing love; my heart rejoices in your salvation. I will sing to the Lord, for he has been good to me.

81

Sing to Jesus

Special One,
you can trust in My unfailing love.
You can have joy because
I have rescued you.
Come and sing thankful songs to Me.
Love,
~ Jesus

1. How did I rescue you?
2. Why can you have joy because I rescued you?
3. How can you sing thankful songs to Me?

Romans 10:9 (NIV)

If you declare with your mouth, "Jesus is Lord,"
and believe in your heart that God raised him from
the dead, you will be saved.

82

Jesus Is Alive

Trusting One,
if you say out loud that Jesus is Lord,
and believe in your heart that
I raised Jesus from death,
you will be saved.
This was all because of
My great love for you.
You are that precious to me.

~ God

1. Do you believe in your heart that you want Me to be in charge of your life?
2. Why is it important to say what you believe out loud?
3. How did I raise Jesus from death?

Psalm 131:3

Israel, put your hope in the Lord
both now and forever.

You Are My Beloved

Dear One,
you can put your hope
in Me now and forever.
You are My beloved.
Love,
~ God

ᄽᄽᄽᄽᄽᄽᄽ

1. What does it mean to put your hope in someone or something?
2. What does it mean to be someone's "beloved"?
3. Why is it good to put your hope in Me?

Romans 8:38–39

I am absolutely sure that not even death or life can separate us from God's love. Not even angels or demons, the present or the future, or any powers can separate us. Not even the highest places or the lowest, or anything else in all creation can separate us. Nothing at all can ever separate us from God's love. That because of what Christ Jesus our Lord has done.

84

Nothing Can Separate Us

Most Loved One,
please know that absolutely nothing
can separate you from My love.
My forever love was made possible
by My sacrifice!
My Father and I love you!

~ Jesus

❦❦❦❦❦❦❦

1. What does it mean to be separated from something?
2. How do you feel knowing you can't be separated from My love no matter what?
3. How do you know you have My love?

Colossians 1:9

That's why we have not stopped praying for you. We have been praying for you since the day we heard about you. We keep asking God to fill you with the knowledge of what he wants. We pray he will give you the wisdom and understanding that the Spirit gives.

85

My Wisdom for You

My child,
ask God to fill you with His wisdom
and the knowledge of what
He wants for you,
so you can understand
how God works.
He will answer if you ask.
I promise.

~ *Jesus*

⌒⌒⌒⌒⌒⌒⌒

1. What does it mean to have wisdom?
2. Why would it be good to have My wisdom?
3. Do you think My plan for you is the very best
   there is?

Psalm 17:8 (NIV)

Keep me as the apple of your eye; hide me in the shadow of your wings.

86

The Apple of My Eye

Dearest Child,
you are the apple of My eye.
Like a mother bird, I will hide
and protect you under My wings.
Love,
~ Your Heavenly Father

～⚬⚬⚬⚬⚬⚬⚬⚬⚬

1. What does it mean to be the apple of someone's eye?
2. How can I hide and protect you under My wings?
3. When are times you would like Me to protect you?

John 1:43 (NIV)

The next day Jesus decided to leave for Galilee. Finding Philip, he said to him, "Follow me."

87

Follow Me

Child,
just as I asked Philip to follow Me,
I am asking you to follow Me too.
I delight in you!
All my love,
~ Jesus

❧❦❧❦❧❦❧❦❧❦❧

1. Why do you think Philip followed Me?
2. How can you follow Me?
3. How do you feel knowing that I delight in you?

Isaiah 54:13

I will teach all your children. And they will enjoy great peace.

Come Learn from Me

My Child,
I want to teach you
and give you great peace.
Love,
~ God

❧❧❧❧❧❧❧❧❧

1. What are some ways I teach you?
2. What does it mean to have peace?
3. Why is it good to have peace?

1 John 4:19–21

We love because he loved us first. Suppose someone claims to love God but hates a brother or sister. Then they are a liar. They don't love their brother or sister, whom they have seen. So they can't love God whom they haven't seen. Here is the command God has given us. Anyone who loves God must also love their brother and sister.

89

Endless Love

Dear One,
you can love because I first loved you.
You show your love for Me
by loving the people around you.
If you love Me,
it is necessary for you to love others.
My love for you never ends.

~ *Jesus*

---

1. How did I first love you?
2. What are ways you can love the people around you?
3. Is it always easy to love the people you know?

John 14:27 (NIV)

Peace I leave with you; my peace I give you. I do
not give to you as the world gives. Do not let your
hearts be troubled and do not be afraid.

90

Peace of Mind and Heart

My Child,
I have given you a gift.
This gift is peace of mind and heart.
And the peace I give is a gift
the world cannot give.
So, don't be troubled or afraid.
All my love,

~ *Jesus*

❄❄❄❄❄❄❄

1. What does it mean to have peace of mind and heart?
2. Why can't the world you live in give you this same peace?
3. How can My peace help you not be troubled or afraid?

Psalm 108:4 (NIV)

For great is your love, higher than the heavens;
your faithfulness reaches to the skies.

91

How Great My Love

Dear Child,
My great love for you
is higher than the heavens.
My faithfulness to you
reaches to the skies.
Love always,
~ God

---

1. How high is "higher than the heavens"?
2. How high is it when something reaches all the way to the sky?
3. Did you know that My love and help are that big?

Psalm 30:11–12

You turned my loud crying into dancing. You removed my clothes of sadness and dressed me with joy. So my heart will sing your praises. I can't keep silent. Lord, my God, I will praise you forever.

92

Come and Dance

Dear One,
I can turn your crying
into dancing and
I can give you happiness,
because I love you!
Sing to Me with songs of praise,
because of how much I love you.

~ God

1. How do I turn your crying into dancing?
2. Are there times after you pray to Me that you feel happier?
3. What songs do you like to sing to Me?

Isaiah 25:8

He will swallow up death forever. The Lord and
King will wipe away the tears from everyone's face.
He will remove the shame of his people from the
whole earth. The Lord has spoken.

93

No More Tears

My Child,
When you come to heaven,
I will wipe away any tears
from your face
and I will take away any
shame you feel.
I love you.
~ God

---

1. What does shame feel like?
2. When have you felt shamed?
3. Are you happy that I promise you will never be shamed or sad in heaven?

Psalm 118:24 (NIV)

This is the day the Lord has made; let us rejoice and be glad in it.

Let's Celebrate

My Dear Child,
this is the day I have made.
Let's celebrate and
be happy for it together.
Love,
~ God

1. Do I make every day?
2. What does it mean to celebrate something?
3. How can you celebrate and be happy for each day?

Psalm 138:7

Trouble is all around me, but you keep me alive. You reach out your hand to put a stop to the anger of my enemies. With your powerful right hand you save me.

95

Reaching for You

Dear One,
even if you find yourself
in the middle of a bunch of trouble,
I will help you and
reach out to you to save you.
~ *Your God, who loves you.*

꧂꧂꧂꧂꧂꧂

1. When have you found yourself in the middle of a bunch of trouble?
2. Did you wish someone would reach out to help you?
3. How can I reach out to save you?

John 15:13

No one has greater love than the one who gives their life for their friends.

96

No Greater Love

Special One,
I loved you so much
that I died for you.
You are My special child
and My special friend.
Love always and forever,
~ *Jesus*

꧁꧂꧁꧂꧁꧂꧁꧂

1. How did I die for you?
2. Why did I need to die?
3. Are you glad I am now alive and loving you?

John 16:24 (NIV)

Until now you have not asked for anything in my name. Ask and you will receive, and your joy will be complete.

Ask Me Anything

Dear Child,
ask Me anything using My name and
you will receive My very best for you.
You will experience lots of joy!
Love,
~ Jesus

1. In what ways do you use My name when you pray?
2. Can you trust Me to give you what is best?
3. What brings you lots of joy?

Colossians 1:11 (NIV)

. . . being strengthened with all power according to his glorious might so that you may have great endurance and patience . . .

My Magnificent Power

Child,
I want you to know My will,
so you can draw strength
from My magnificent power.
I want to share My power with you,
so you can have great endurance
and patience.
Love,
~ Jesus

1. What does it mean to have great endurance?
2. Do you think My power can help you keep going when life is hard?
3. How powerful do you think My magnificent power is?

Psalm 62:8

*Trust in him at all times, you people. Tell him all
your troubles. God is our place of safety.*

99

Pour Out Your Heart

Dear One,
you can pour out your
heart to Me always.
You can trust in Me because
I am a safe place for you.
I am always safe.
~ God

~~~~~~~~~~~

1. How can you pour out your heart to Me?
2. What would you like to talk to Me about?
3. Why am I a safe place for you?

Psalm 88:1--2

Lord, you are the God who saves me. Day and night I cry out to you. Please hear my prayer. Pay attention to my cry for help.

100

Cry Out to Me

Dearest Child,
I am the One who hears
your cry and saves you.
You can always call out to Me
and I will hear you.
I promise with love.
~ *God*

---

1. When do you call out to Me?
2. Why can you count on Me to hear you?
3. What would you like to call out to Me about right now?

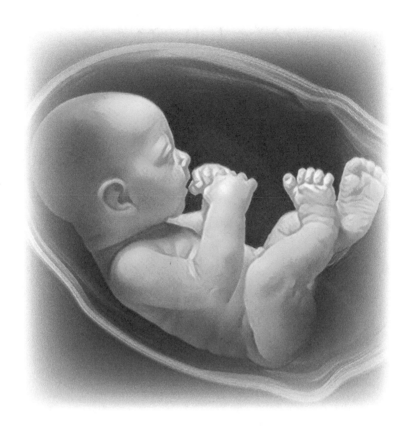

Jeremiah 1:5 (NIV)

Before I formed you in the womb I knew you.

101

I Have Always Known You

Most Special Child,
before you were even born,
I knew all about you.
I have special plans just for you.
I will love you always.
~ *Your Loving Heavenly Father*

꧁꧂꧁꧂꧁꧂꧁꧂꧁꧂

1. How could I know you before you were born?
2. Would you like to know My special plans for you?
3. How can I let you know those special plans?